Contents

Welcome to Kenya

Kenya is a **tropical** country on the east coast of Africa. More than 40 million people live in the **Republic** of Kenya. The country has two official languages—English and Swahili. There are over 40 native tribes, or groups, as well as immigrants from other countries. Each group has special **customs** that make up the unique culture of Kenya.

Kenya's capital city is Nairobi. The name *Nairobi* means "the place of cold water" in Swahili.

Cultural traditions, or customs, have been practiced for thousands of years by Kenya's native groups. Many holidays include religious customs, or focus on special events in Kenya's history. Celebrations in Kenya often include traditional songs and dances.

Did You Know?
There are special dances for different occasions in Kenya. In the photo above, women in the Samburu tribe are performing a welcome dance.

Birthdays and Weddings

It is a custom to name children after **ancestors**. Kenyans believe the ancestor's spirit will live on in the child. As a child grows, birthdays are celebrated with a special meal and cake. A traditional Kenyan sponge cake is called *Mkate wa Mayai*, which means "bread of eggs." It is made with eggs, sugar, baking powder, flour, and spices. It is a popular traditional cake for celebrations in Kenya.

When Kikuyu girls are born, they are traditionally given one of nine names from a story about the creation of the world.

Kenyan weddings can be traditional or modern or a mix of both. Traditional weddings run for several days of singing, dancing, and feasting. The bride and groom are married in front of friends and family. Different tribes have different wedding clothes and traditions. Swahili brides have their skin tattooed with **henna** designs. The Samburu cross wooden sticks during the ceremony to bless the marriage with strong roots. In more modern weddings, Kenyan brides prefer white wedding gowns like those worn in North American weddings.

This couple wears the traditional wedding clothes of the Samburu.

Did You Know?
In the Maasai culture, the bride's father gives his blessing on the marriage by spitting on the bride's chest and head.

Children's Activities

After children have completed their chores for the day, they spend the evenings with family and friends. Everyone gathers together to tell stories, sing, and play games. There are many traditional games and activities in Kenya. Many families cannot afford to buy toys for their children. Instead, children play with items from their everyday lives. Stones, sticks, trees, and even animals are used in the games children play.

These children are playing the ancient game *Mancala*. Players drop stones clockwise into 12 small pits in the ground. The player who ends up with the most stones in the *kalaha*, or right-hand pit, wins.

Children in Kenya also enjoy playing sports such as soccer (which they call football), cricket, and other outdoor running sports. Some also participate in traditional dancing and singing. Young performers travel to take part in competitions between tribal groups. The competitions help keep Kenya's culture alive. One national competition called the Kenyan Music Festival takes place among high school students every August.

Did You Know?
Kenyan Wilson Kipsang is a record-holding **marathon** runner. Many long-distance runners from Kenya have won medals at world championships.

9

Happy New Year!

New Year's Eve falls on December 31. Kenyans celebrate with food, friends, and fireworks. Some people gather for a meal of traditional African dishes. *Sukuma Wiki* is a dish made up of leafy green vegetables fried with onions and tomatoes. *Ugali*, shown here on the left with potatoes, is another popular Kenyan dish. It is like a thick porridge made with white cornmeal.

Dhow racing is a New Year's Day tradition on Lamu Island. A dhow is an ancient style of sailboat.

New Year's Day is celebrated January 1 with a public holiday for all Kenyans. Families usually spend the day together. In Mombasa, people attend beach parties to celebrate the first day of the new year. People travel from long distances to enjoy New Year's Day at the beach.

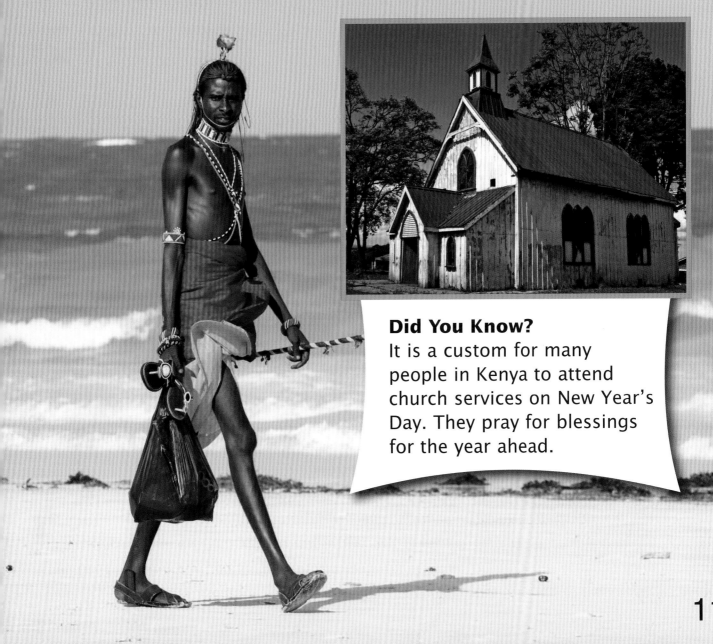

Did You Know?
It is a custom for many people in Kenya to attend church services on New Year's Day. They pray for blessings for the year ahead.

Good Friday and Easter

More than 80 percent of Kenyans follow the **Christian** religion. Easter is a time when Christians remember the death of Jesus Christ and his return to life. No matter which religion they follow, all Kenyans get a public holiday on Good Friday and Easter Monday. Easter falls on different days in March or April each year.

Some Christians in Kenya act out the last day of Jesus Christ's life. They carry a huge wooden cross through the streets while others watch.

On Good Friday and Easter Sunday, families attend church services. There are often bonfires, singing, parades, and the ringing of church bells. Feasting and celebrating with family are traditional Easter activities in Kenya.

Did You Know?
Palm Sunday occurs one week before Easter. Children march through villages waving palm leaves, shouting "Christ is risen!"

Labor Day

Kenyans celebrate Labor Day on May 1. In the past, many workers suffered due to poor working conditions and long work days. People fought for the right to limit the work day to eight hours. Labor Day is a public holiday that celebrates Kenya's hardworking people.

Kenyan families attend picnics and parades on Labor Day. Sometimes they enjoy fireworks as part of the celebration.

Many Kenyans are farmers. Some of the crops they grow include coffee, tea, corn, wheat, **sisal**, sugar cane, fruits, and vegetables. Kenyans believe that hard work brings reward. *Kula Jasho* is a Kenyan phrase said with pride, which means "to eat from your labor."

Did You Know?
The Kikuyu tribe celebrates the beginning of the planting season with ceremonial dances performed by some of the tribe's warriors, followed by a feast.

15

Madaraka Day

Madaraka Day is a national holiday that is celebrated on June 1. Kenya became a British colony in 1920. Britain ruled Kenya for many years, but Kenyans wanted to take back control of their own country. In the battle against Britain, thousands of Kenyans died.

In 1963, Kenyans won back the right to rule their own country. Kenyans are shown here celebrating Madaraka Day in the streets of Nairobi.

Girl guides in a parade salute the country's president.

Madaraka is a Swahili word that means "**self-determination**." The people of Kenya worked together to win their country's freedom. Today, the national motto of Kenya is "*Harambee*" which means "pull together." To honor those who lost their lives in the struggle, people celebrate Madaraka Day. It marks the first victory that led to the country's **independence** later that year.

Did You Know?
The leader of the fight for self rule was Dedan Kimathi. He is a national hero in Kenya.

Jamhuri Day (Independence Day)

Jamhuri Day is Kenya's national Independence Day. Celebrated on December 12, Jamhuri is a Swahili word that means "republic." The people of Kenya celebrate the day they became the Republic of Kenya. Six months after Kenya won the right to rule itself, it became an independent country.

These Kikuyu people are taking part in a Jamhuri Day parade.

Jamhuri Day is a national holiday. Celebrations include family gatherings, political speeches, dancing, and parades. Feasting on traditional Kenyan foods, such as corn, tomato stew, and roasted meat, is an important part of the celebration.

Did You Know?
The colors of Kenya's flag tell the story of its people. Black stands for heritage, red represents Kenya's fight for independence, green stands for crops, and white is a symbol of peace. The shield and spears show Kenya's strength in protecting its freedom.

19

Camel Derby and Rhino Charge

One of the most adventurous cultural events in Kenya is the International Camel Derby. It is held each August. Riders race camels about 26 miles (42 kilometers) across the desert to the finish line. The race attracts riders from all over the world.

Camels have been an important part of the **nomadic** lifestyle of Kenya's Samburu tribe for hundreds of years.

Did You Know?
Many reserves have been set up across Kenya to protect wild spaces for animals. Some offer cultural tours by tribespeople.

Another event is the Rhino Charge off-road race. Drivers race vehicles across the countryside to raise money for a charity called Rhino Ark. The charity protects the **endangered** black rhinoceros population in Kenya's Aberdare National Park.

Muslim Holidays

Over ten percent of Kenyans follow the **Muslim** religion of **Islam**. Eid al-Fitr is a celebration at the end of Ramadan. Ramadan is an important month-long religious observance. Muslims must not eat, drink, or smoke during daylight hours for the month of Ramadan to show their devotion to their faith. On Eid al-Fitr, friends and family gather to celebrate the end of fasting with a three-day feast of traditional sweet foods, along with music and gifts.

Eid is an Arabic word meaning "festivity."

Did You Know?
Islam arrived in Kenya hundreds of years ago when Arab traders from India came to do business with the African people.

Kenya's *Maulidi* celebration is held each year on the island of Lamu. Maulidi is an Islamic festival. Muslims celebrate the birth of the **prophet** Muhammad. During the month of Maulidi, they organize events to build community spirit. These may include donkey races, poetry readings, and swimming activities.

Tribal Customs

Kenya's many tribal cultures have their own clothing, music, and ceremonies. Music and dance are especially important in ceremonies that celebrate events in people's lives.

The largest tribe in Kenya is the Kikuyu. Traditional Kikuyu dancers wear bright colors and face paint when they perform.

Did You Know?
In the Maasai tribe, young boys spend ten years learning to be warriors. When they have completed their training, a celebration is held. Called *Morani*, these warriors perform a jumping dance competition to win the attention of young women. When it is over, the Morani are free to marry and begin a family.

Maasai women dress in long red sheets of cloth called *shuka* as they celebrate marriages and **coming-of-age rituals**. They wrap the sheets around their bodies and wear handmade beaded jewelry. Making jewelry is a daily part of life for women and girls.

Mashujaa Day (Heroes Day)

Mashujaa Day is a national public holiday that falls on October 20. The Swahili word *Mashujaa* means "heroes." Kenyans celebrate their national heroes with parades, church services, festivities, and an annual speech by the country's president.

Uhuru Memorial Garden Park features the towering Nyayo Monument to Kenya's Independence Day.

Mashujaa Day began as a day to celebrate and honor Kenya's first president, Mzee Jomo Kenyatta (shown at right). Mashujaa Day was originally called Kenyatta Day in his honor. The name was changed to Mashujaa Day to pay respect to all of Kenya's heroes, past and present.

Mombasa Carnival

Each November, the city of Mombasa hosts the most popular festival in Kenya. At the Mombasa Carnival, Kenyan culture is celebrated with parades featuring decorated floats, music, and dances. People dress in brightly colored costumes. Souvenirs and foods from a variety of cultures are sold at stalls along the parade routes.

Many talented artists and entertainers thrill visitors at the Mombasa Carnival.

The Mombasa Carnival brings people from different tribes together in the spirit of celebration. It is a chance for Kenyans to learn more about each other through songs, dances, and traditional foods.

29

Christmas and Boxing Day

Christmas is celebrated on December 25. Boxing Day follows on December 26. It is known as *Krismusi* in Kenya. Many Kenyans attend church services to celebrate Christ's birth. Homes and businesses are decorated with bells on palm trees and fake snow. Kenyans who can afford to exchange gifts give items that are useful or affordable. Soap, clothing, and schoolbooks are common gifts.

Some men must work and live in a big city to make money. A Christmas visit is often the only opportunity all year for this Maasai father to see his wife and child.

On Boxing Day, Kenyans look forward to having a day of rest. Both Christmas and Boxing Day are national public holidays. Friends and family celebrate with a feast of roasted meats and rice pudding. They play music, sing, and dance. It is a joyful celebration!

Did You Know?
Nyama choma, which means "burnt meat," is a popular dish in Kenya that is often served at Christmas. The main ingredient is roasted meat—usually goat or beef. The meal is served with beer for the adults, and fruit juice or soda for the children.

Glossary

ancestors Family members from the past

Christian Someone who follows the teachings of Jesus Christ, whom they believe to be the Son of God

coming-of-age rituals Religious or traditional actions performed when children reach adulthood

customs Practices based on religious or historical beliefs

endangered Describing plants or animals that are in danger of dying out completely in the wild

henna A reddish brown dye used to color hair or decorate a body

independence A country's ability to rule itself

Islam A religion practiced by Muslims that follows one God through the teachings of the prophet Muhammad

marathon A running race that is about 26 miles (42 kilometers) long

Muslim People who follow Islam and the teachings of the prophet Muhammad

nomadic Having no permanent home and moving from place to place

prophet A member of a religious group who delivers messages believed to come from God

republic A country ruled by leaders put in place by the voting public

self-determination The freedom to make your own choices

sisal A plant used to make rope, twine, and carpets

tropical Hot and humid

Index